HOW TO MAKE

POP-UPS

HOW TO MAKE
POP-UPS

BY JOAN IRVINE

ILLUSTRATED BY BARBARA REID

MORROW JUNIOR BOOKS / NEW YORK

Text copyright © 1987 by Joan Irvine
Illustrations copyright © 1987 by Barbara Reid
First published in Canada in 1987 by Kids Can Press, 585½ Bloor
Street West, Toronto, Ontario, CANADA M6G 1K5

Printed in the United States of America.
1 2 3 4 5 6 7 8 9 10

Library of Congress Cataloging-in-Publication Data

Irvine, Joan, 1951-
    How to make pop-ups/by Joan Irvine; illustrated by Barbara
Reid.
        p.   cm.
    Summary: Offers step-by-step instructions for making pop-up cards,
books, sculptures, and other objects out of materials found at home.
    ISBN 0-688-07902-4 (pbk.). ISBN 0-688-07903-2 (lib. bdg.)
    1. Paper work—Juvenile literature.   2. Paper toy making—Juvenile
literature.   3. Creative activities and seat work—Juvenile
literature.   [1. Paperwork.   2. Handicraft.]   I. Reid, Barbara,
ill.   II. Title.   III. Title: Pop-ups.
TT870.I77 1988
745.54—dc19

This book is dedicated both to my family — Steven, Seth and Elly — and to the hundreds of school children whom I have taught who know me as The Pop-up Lady.

Contents

Acknowledgements

I would like to acknowledge the support of the Ontario Arts Council through the program Creative Artists in Schools. As a result of receiving Ontario Arts Council grants and teaching hundreds of students the art of making pop-up books in twelve schools throughout Grey and Bruce Counties, I have had the opportunity to explore and develop pop-up construction with many children.

Thank you to the many children in schools who tested and invented new pop-up techniques.

My own children helped me enormously with sections of the book. A thank you to my husband for his support and patience during the project.

A great thank you goes to my editor, Sarah Swartz, who helped me in rewriting and improving the original manuscript.

Finally, I would like to acknowledge the helpful advice and encouragement of Val Wyatt, Valerie Hussey and Ricky Englander of Kids Can Press.

Introduction

If you've ever seen a pop-up book or card, you'll know how special they are. Suddenly a figure comes alive by leaping out at you or moving across the page. Pop-ups are full of surprises, magic and fun.

This book will show you how to make your very own pop-ups. You may need a birthday card for a friend or some party invitations. You may want to make your own cards for Mother's Day, Valentine's Day, Halloween or other holidays. Your family and friends will love them, and you will have the satisfaction of knowing you made them yourself. Using the ideas in this book, you can even make a centrepiece or a free-standing object for a school project.

By making your own pop-ups, you will be carrying on a very long tradition. In the 1700s, "novelty books" with flaps, peepholes and cut-outs were produced to amuse children. In the 1840s, greeting cards with simple pop-ups became popular. Valentine cards were made with flaps that opened to show a message or scene.

Making pop-ups is easy. First, choose a design that works best for your message. This book will give you suggestions for different types of pop-ups. You don't need to follow all the ideas in one section before you start another section. After a while, you will find you are inventing your own pop-up ideas.

Next, carefully follow the instructions for cutting and folding. Your first pop-up will probably be the hardest to make, but with practice you will become an expert. Remember to take your time and be patient. And most important of all, have fun!

Materials

To make your pop-ups, you will need the following materials.

- *Paper* For cards that will last, use heavy paper like construction paper or light bristol board. Lighter weight paper can be used for pop-ups that don't get much wear and tear. The instructions will tell you when to use bristol board or cardboard.

- *Scissors* A sharp pair of scissors with pointed ends are good for cutting paper. Remember to use all cutting equipment with care.

- *Cutting blade* An Olfa touch knife, an X-acto knife or any other kind of craft knife is useful for making a cut in the middle of a page. Ask an adult to help when you need to use a cutting blade.

- *Ruler* Use a ruler for measurements given in the instructions. A metal ruler will help you make crisp folds and guide your cutting blade.

- *Glue* With light paper, use a glue stick. With heavy paper, use white glue. Always apply glue sparingly and keep glue clear of all moving parts of your pop-up. When you glue two pieces of paper together, a strip of glue on each edge is usually enough.

- *Pencil, markers, crayons, coloured pencils, paints* Use an erasable pencil for marking measurements and for designing your drawings. Then go over your pencil drawings with colour.

- *Brass fasteners* These fasteners, which are used for moving circles, are available at stationery or business supply stores. Make sure to use a small size.

- *String, rubber bands, fabrics, buttons, ribbons, gift wrap, feathers, magazines* These materials and others can be glued to your pop-ups as decorations.

Symbols and Definitions

The following symbols and definitions will be useful to you when you use this book.

- Flap — a small piece of paper that hangs loose
- Tab — a small paper insert that can be glued or pulled
- Slot — an opening that works like a pocket
- Spring — a folded device that makes an object pop up
- Sliding strip — a small piece of paper that helps an object to move
- Mountain fold — an upward fold, shaped like a mountain
- Valley fold — a downward fold, shaped like a valley
- Accordian fold — an up-down-up fold or a down-up-down fold, shaped like a fan

 • Fold line

 • Cut line

 • Draw

 • Colour

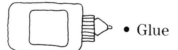 • Glue

 • Measure

Tips for Folding and Scoring

To make a straight fold on heavy paper, score the paper first. Scoring means making a crease on your paper along the line to be folded. Lay a metal ruler near the line to be folded. Then carefully run the blunt end of a pair of scissors or a ball-point pen without ink along the fold line. Some people score their paper by running a fingernail across the fold line. When you fold your paper, remember to press firmly.

Tips for Cutting

You will need a sharp pair of scissors for most activities in this book. If you are making a cut in the middle of a page, use a pair of pointed scissors to puncture one of the corners of the cut line before cutting.

A cutting blade, such as an Olfa touch knife or an X-acto knife, works best to make a cut in the middle of a page. Be careful when using a cutting blade. Adult supervision is recommended.

When you use a cutting blade, a metal ruler will help you to guide the knife down the side of the ruler. Always put a board or a thick piece of cardboard under your work, so that you don't damage your work space.

Tips for Measuring

All measurements are given in both metric and imperial systems. When you follow the instructions for making a pop-up, start with one system and stay with it for the whole activity. Measurements differ slightly from system to system.

Part One   Push and Pop Out

Would you like to make a talking creature or a valentine for your friend? You will find the ideas in Part One.

With push and pop-out cards, you will be cutting, folding and pushing a shape through to the other side of your paper. Your shape will pop out from the middle or the top of the page.

Some push and pop-out cards have the same kind of cuts and folds. The pop-up strip and the cage have straight, horizontal cuts. The triangle pop-up, the nose, the valentine and the opening flower have triangle shaped push-out areas.

Tips

- After you fold your paper in half, always cut on the *folded edge*.
- After you cut your paper, make *firm* folds by going over the fold lines with your thumb and index finger.
- It is easier to push your cut shape through to the other side, if you hold your paper like a tent.
- If you close your card and press firmly, the cut shape will remain pushed through to the other side of the paper.
- When you glue the inside and outside cards together, apply glue only to the outer edges of the inside card.
- Never apply glue near the pop-up shape.

Make a Pop-up Strip

1 Take two pieces of paper, each 21.5 cm x 28 cm (8½ in. x 11 in.). Fold each paper in half. Put one paper aside.

2 In the middle of the *folded edge* of the other paper, mark two dots, 1 cm (¼ in.) apart.

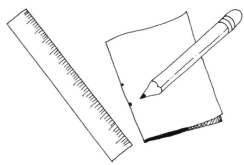

3 Starting at the dots, draw two parallel lines towards the edge of the paper. Each line should be 2.5 cm (1 in.) long.

4 Cut the lines starting from the folded edge.

5 Fold the cut strip back and then fold it forward again.

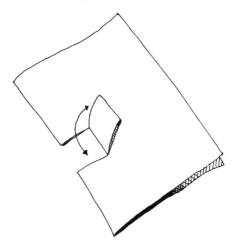

6 Open your card and hold it like a tent. Push the strip through to the other side of your card. Close the card and press firmly. Open to see the pop-up strip.

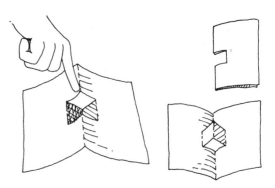

7 Draw a person or animal on a sheet of paper. The figure can be a little taller and wider than your strip. Colour in the figure. Then cut it out.

8 Apply glue on one side of the strip. Place the figure on the glue.

9 Now glue your card to the paper you put aside, which now becomes the outside of your card. When you open your card, the little cut-out figure will pop up.

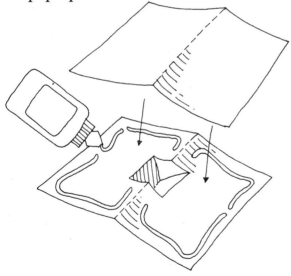

10 Decorate the front and inside of your card.

More Pop-up Strips

House Shape

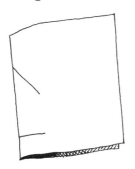

Egg Shape

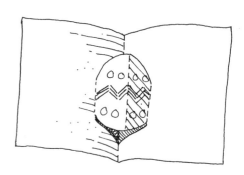

Butterfly Shape

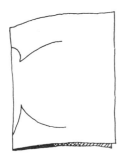

You can make more than one strip in the middle of your card. Each strip can be a different size.

You can also stick figures on both sides of your strip.

Have fun by adding more paper to your strips.

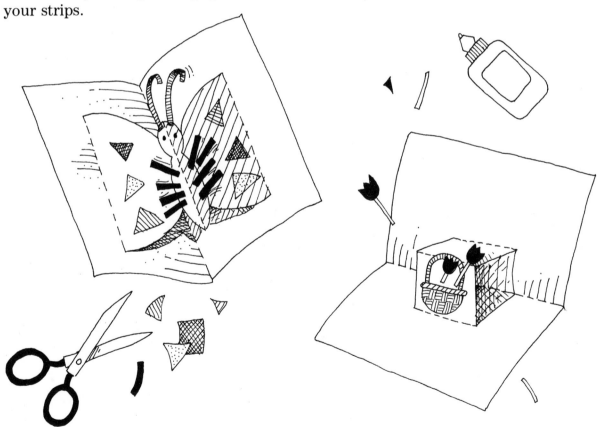

Triangle Pop-ups

1 Take two pieces of paper, each 21.5 cm x 28 cm (8½ in. x 11 in.). Fold each paper in half. Put one aside.

2 Place the other paper so that the folded edge is on your left. Fold the top corner to make a triangle.

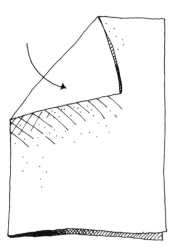

3 Unfold the triangle and open the card. You will see an upside-down triangle at the top of your page. Pull the triangle towards you. Press the fold lines in the opposite direction of the original folds, so that the triangle points forward.

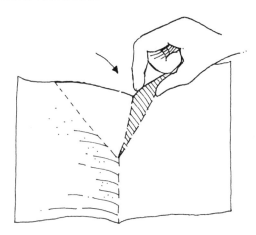

4 When you close the card, it will look like this:

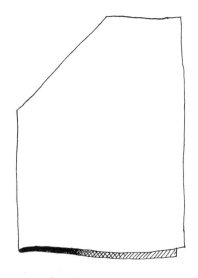

5 Apply glue to the outside of your card. Glue it to the paper you put aside, which now becomes the outside of your card. *Make sure you do not apply glue in the pop-up triangle area.*

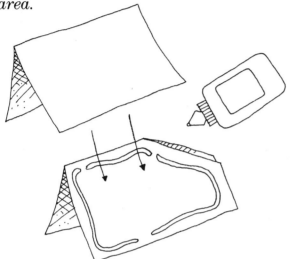

6 Take a piece of paper that is 5 cm x 7 cm (2 in. x 2¾ in.). Draw a figure on this paper. It could be a person, an animal or an object. Colour it and cut it out.

7 Fold the figure in half vertically. Apply glue on the bottom area of the back of your figure. Place the figure on the triangle, so that the folds match and the top part of the figure is above your card.

8 Now decorate the front and inside of your card.

Make a Talking Mouth

1 Take two pieces of paper, each 21.5 cm x 28 cm (8½ in. x 11 in.). Fold each paper in half. Put one aside.

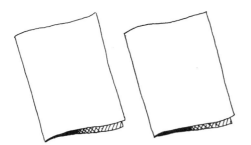

2 On the other, put a dot in approximately the centre of the folded edge.

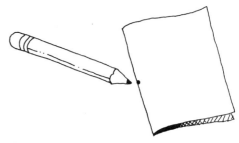

3 Draw a 5 cm (2 in.) line from the dot towards the outer edge.

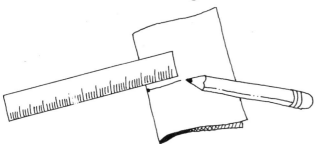

4 Starting at the folded edge, cut on the line.

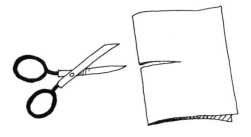

5 Fold back the flaps to form two triangles.

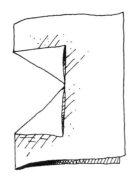

6 Open up the flaps again. Open the whole page.

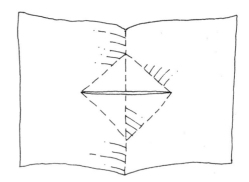

7 Now comes the tricky part! Hold your paper, so that it looks like a tent. Put your finger on the top triangle and push down. Pinch the two folded edges of the top triangle, so that the triangle is pushed through to the other side of the paper.

8 Put your finger on the bottom triangle and do the same thing. The top and bottom triangles will now be pushed out to form a mouth inside the card. When you open and close your card, the mouth will look like it is talking. When your card is closed, it will look like this:

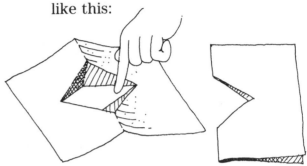

9 Draw a monster, a person or an animal around your mouth.

10 Glue the inside and outside cards together. *Do not apply glue in the area of the pop-up mouth.* You now have a cover for your card.

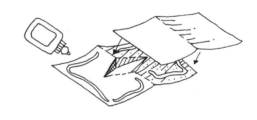

Other Ideas

Your card can also be a centrepiece for a table, if you use heavy paper.

1 Draw a jagged line, instead of a straight line, for the talking mouth. Your figure will now have teeth.

2 Draw a head and body around the mouth. Make sure the body is wider than the head, so that your figure can stand.

3 Cut around the figure's head and body to make a centrepiece.

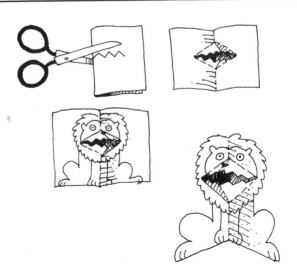

Make a Pop-up Valentine

1 Take two pieces of paper, each 21.5 cm x 28 cm (8½ in. x 11 in.). Fold each paper in half. Put one aside.

2 Place the other paper so that the folded edge is on your left. Fold the top corner to make a large triangle.

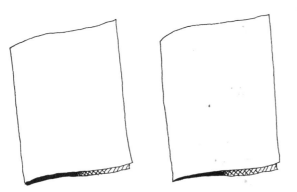

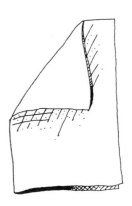

3 Fold back the triangle. Draw the top part of half a heart from the folded edge to the triangle fold.

4 Cut the top part of the valentine, stopping at the triangle fold mark.

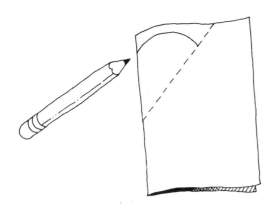

5 Open the card and pull the valentine towards you. Press the fold lines so that the valentine points forward.

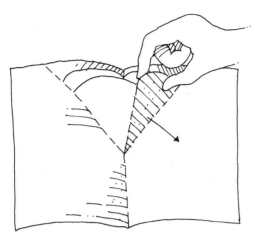

6 Colour the valentine.

7 Apply glue to the outside of your card. Glue it to the paper you put aside. *Do not apply glue in the area of the pop-up heart.*

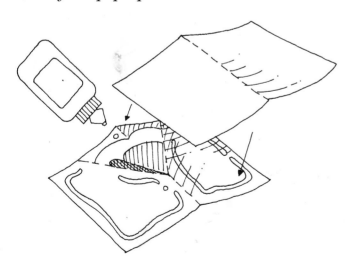

8 Decorate the front of your card.

Make a Nose

1 Take two pieces of paper, each 21.5 cm x 28 cm (8½ in. x 11 in.). Fold each paper in half. Put one aside.

2 Place the other paper so that the folded edge is on your left. Fold the bottom corner to make a large triangle.

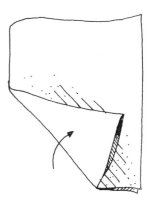

3 Fold back the triangle. Draw a curved line from the folded edge to the triangle fold. Then cut along this curved line, stopping at the triangle fold mark.

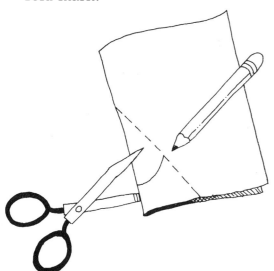

4 Open the card. You will see a nose shape. Pull the nose towards you. Press the fold lines, so that the nose points towards you.

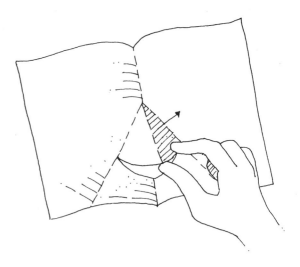

5 Glue the inside and outside cards together. *Do not apply glue in the area of the pop-up nose.*

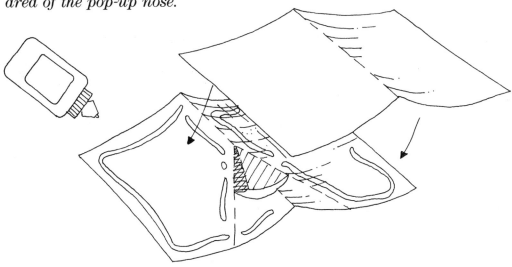

6 Draw a face around the nose. Decorate the front of your card.

More Triangle Folds

Vase of Flowers

1 Make a pop-up valentine shape. (See page 24.)

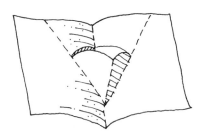

2 Draw, colour and cut out several flowers.

3 Attach paper flowers to the inside of the valentine. Colour the valentine vase.

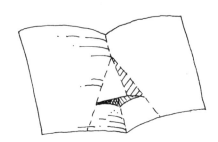

Angel

1 Make a pop-up nose shape. (See page 26.)

2 Draw a head with a halo at the top of this triangle shape. Add wings and hands. Colour the triangle. It becomes the angel's dress.

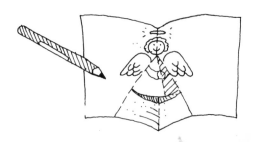

3 Draw, colour and cut out two feet. Attach feet to the bottom of the triangle.

Umbrella

1 Make a triangle fold at the bottom of a piece of paper.

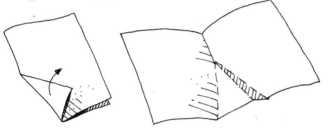

2 Colour the triangle so that it looks like an umbrella.

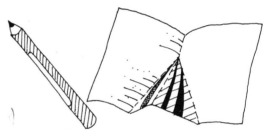

3 Draw, colour and cut out a handle. Glue the handle to the inside of the bottom triangle at one side of the fold line.

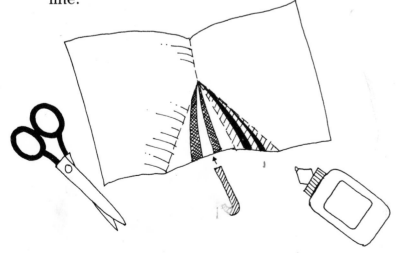

Make an Open Flower

1 Take two pieces of paper, each 21.5 cm x 28 cm (8½ in. x 11 in.). Fold each paper in half. Put one aside.

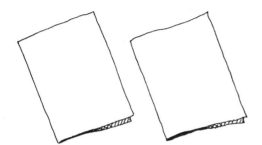

2 Fold the other paper again, so that it is folded in quarters.

3 Open the paper, so that it is folded in half. Take the top left corner and fold to the centre line. Take the bottom left corner and fold to the centre line.

4 Open the paper, so that it is folded in half again.

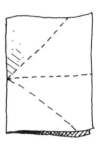

5 With a pencil, draw a curved line from the folded side to the top fold line. Draw a second curved line from the folded side to the bottom fold line. Cut along both curved lines.

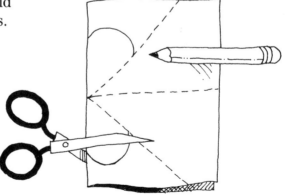

6 Open the paper. You will see two triangles with shapes inside. Pull the shape inside the top triangle towards you. Press the fold lines, so that the shape stands out. Do the same with the shape inside the bottom triangle.

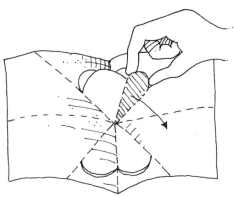

7 When your card is closed, these two shapes, which are the petals of your flower, are tucked inside your card.

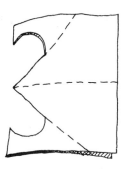

8 Now draw the other petals on your flower. Colour your flower.

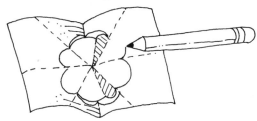

9 Glue the inside and outside cards together. *Do not apply glue in the area of the pop-up petals.*

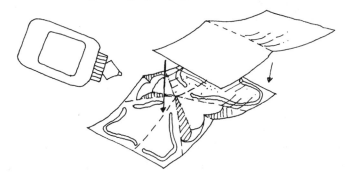

10 Decorate the front and inside of your card.

Let Me Give You A Hug!

1 Take two pieces of paper, each 21.5 cm x 28 cm (8½ in. x 11 in.). Fold each paper in half. Put one aside. Fold the other paper again, so that it is folded in quarters.

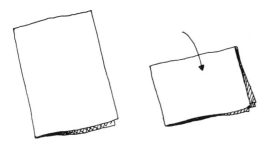

2 Open the paper, so that it is folded in half. Place the folded edge at the top. Starting where the fold lines meet, measure 8 cm (3⅛ in.) on either side of the middle fold line. Mark these points with an x.

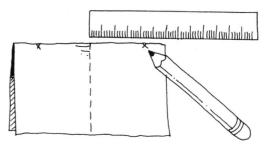

3 From each x, draw a vertical line that is 1.6 cm (⅝ in.) long.

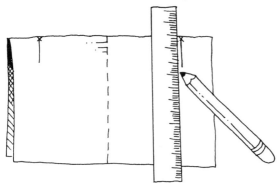

4 At the bottom of each vertical line, draw a horizontal line towards the middle fold, that is 6 cm (2½ in.) long. Cut all the lines.

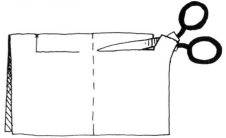

5 Measure .5 cm (⅛ in.) on either side of the middle fold and mark these points with a dot. Draw a dotted line from each dot to the end of each cut line.

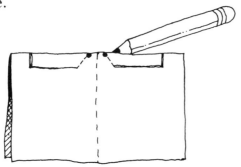

6 Fold the cut pieces towards the centre, along the dotted lines. Press the folds firmly. Fold the cut pieces back again.

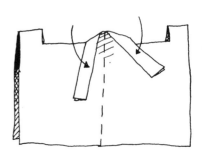

7 Open your paper and hold it like a tent. Push the cut pieces through to the other side of the paper. Press the fold lines in the opposite direction of the original folds, so that your shape is now folded with the peaks towards you. When you open your card, two arms will pop out. When you close your card, it will look like this:

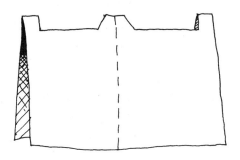

8 Cut out two mittens or hands, each about 3 cm (1¼ in.) long. Fold them down the middle lengthways. Glue them to the arms so that the fold lines match.

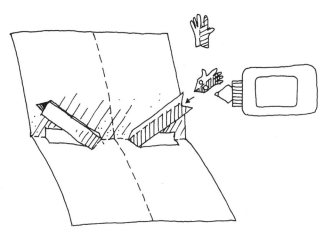

9 Apply glue to the back of your card. Place the card on the paper you have put aside. *Make sure you do not apply glue in the area of the arms.*

10 Draw and colour a body, head and legs for your woman or man. By opening and closing your card, the person will give you a hug.

THANK-YOU!

Make a Cage or a Jail

1 Take two pieces of paper, each 21.5 cm x 28 cm (8½ in. x 11 in.). Fold each paper in half. Put one aside.

2 Along the folded edge of the other paper, draw 12 dots that are 1 cm (⅜ in.) apart. The dots should be in the middle section of the folded edge, beginning 5 cm (2 in.) from the edge of the page.

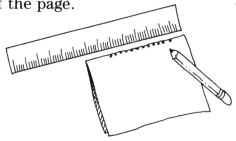

3 Using a ruler, draw a straight line, 7 cm (2¾ in.) long, from the first dot towards the edge of the paper. Draw another line, 7 cm (2¾ in.) long, from the last dot.

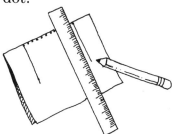

4 From all the other dots, draw lines, 6 cm (2¼ in.) long. Keep them as parallel to each other as possible.

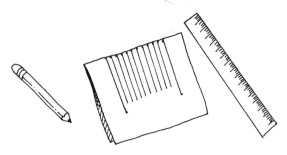

5 Join the long lines with a dotted line. Join the shorter lines with a solid line.

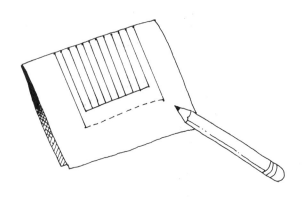

6 Starting at the folded edge, cut all the vertical lines. Shade in each second space that has a solid line across the bottom.

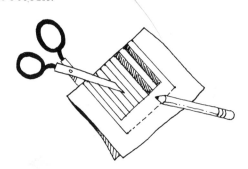

7 Fold the entire inside section along the dotted line. Fold this area back again.

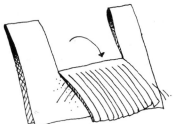

8 Now cut out all the shaded areas.

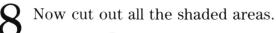

9 Open your paper and hold it like a tent. Push the cut section down in the opposite direction of the fold, so that the bars are pushed through to the other side. Close your card with the cut section inside and press firmly. Open your card. The bars on the cage will stand out.

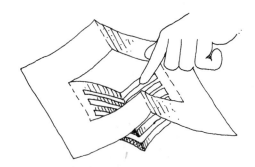

10 Glue the inside and outside papers together. *Do not apply glue in the area of the bars.*

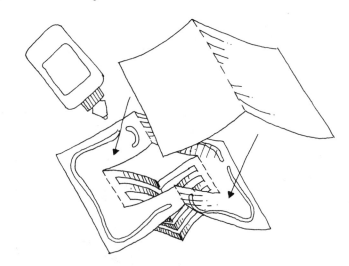

11 Now draw, colour and cut out an animal or person to put in your cage or jail. Make sure to include a tab at the bottom of your figure. Your figure should be glued by its tab inside the cage, facing the bars.

Part Two **Fold and Fit In**

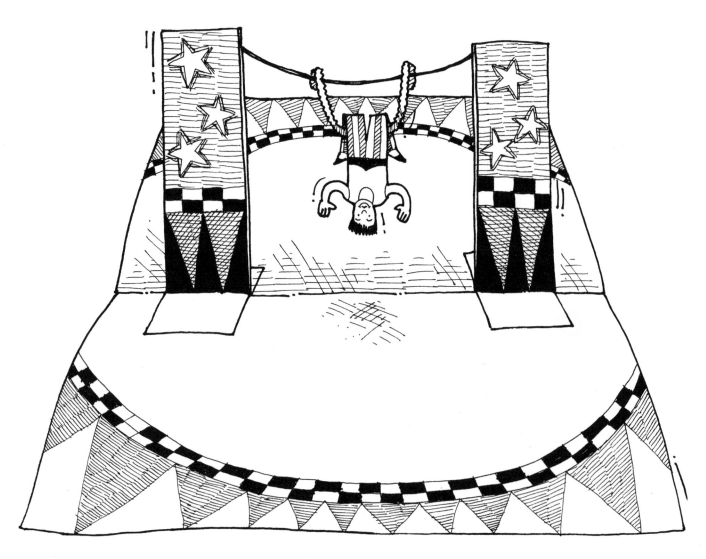

Imagine making a mountain scene with a tiny mountain climber or a little bedroom card with a "Get Well" message. There are many cards that are fun to make in Part Two.

With fold and fit-in cards, you will be cutting and folding a figure or scene. You will then be fitting and gluing it into the middle of the card. The glued figures will pop out when you open your card.

Part Two uses different kinds of folds, such as a mountain fold, a valley fold and an accordion fold. It also uses springs, sometimes called Jacob's Ladder, to make figures pop up.

Some of the cards in this section have similar ways of working. With some ideas, you will be folding a piece of paper a number of times, cutting it and then gluing it into the middle of your card. Sometimes, you will be gluing a structure, such as a mountain, into the middle of the card on the fold line to create an interesting scene.

Tips

- With figures that are cut and folded, such as the cut-out dolls, apply glue on the bottom of the folded piece and place it near the middle fold of your page. Then apply glue on the top and close your card.
- Make sure you allow the glue to dry before you open the card carefully to see your figure pop out.
- Don't be discouraged if your card does not close properly. Gently loosen the glued areas and try placing the folded piece in again more carefully.
- Usually figures will pop up if they are folded in half and have a base that is V-shaped. Make sure that the middle of the V-shaped base is placed directly on the fold line of your paper.

Make a Pop-up Cube or Box

1 Fold a piece of paper, 21.5 cm x 14 cm (8½ in. x 5½ in.), in half. Put it aside. This will be your card.

2 Cut a strip of paper, 4 cm x 16 cm (1½ in. x 6¼ in.). Fold the strip in half lengthways. Then fold the strip in half again. Open the strip and you will have three folds.

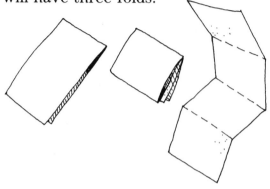

3 Cut a 1 cm (¼ in.) piece off both ends of your strip.

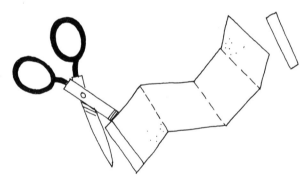

4 Fold the strip on the lines with mountain folds. A *mountain fold* is upward like a mountain ⌂ . You will now have a cube shape.

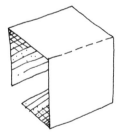

5 Open the cube with the peaks of the folds up. Put glue on both end sections of the strip.

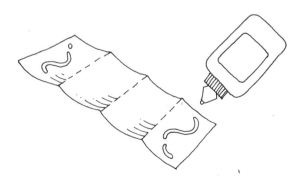

6 Fold the strip into a cube again. Place the cube into the centre of your paper, an equal distance from the top and bottom. Line up the middle fold in the strip with the fold in your paper. The ends of the strip *should not* meet in the middle fold. Make sure that your card opens and closes easily.

7 Draw a figure that is a little taller than one side of your cube. Colour and cut out the figure.

8 Glue it to one side of your cube, making sure that the bottom of your figure is no lower than the bottom of your cube. When your card closes, the figure should be completely inside your card.

9 Decorate the front and inside of your card.

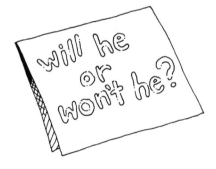

Other Ideas

By using the paper as a vertical card, you can cut out a little figure and glue it *inside* the cube. When you make the figure, cut it out and then fold it in half. Put glue on the front bottom half of the figure. Match the fold lines of the figure with the fold lines of the cube.

Folding Figures

1 Fold a heavy piece of paper, 21.5 cm x 14 cm (8½ in. x 5½ in.), in half. Put it aside. This will be your card.

2 Cut a strip of paper, 17 cm x 7 cm (7 in. x 2¾ in.). Mark the following measurements on the strip, from left to right: 3 cm, 6 cm, 2 cm, and 6 cm (1¼ in., 2½ in., ¾ in., 2½ in.). From each mark, draw a vertical line on your strip. Make sure that sections 2 and 4 are the same size.

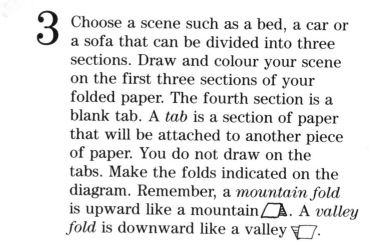

3 Choose a scene such as a bed, a car or a sofa that can be divided into three sections. Draw and colour your scene on the first three sections of your folded paper. The fourth section is a blank tab. A *tab* is a section of paper that will be attached to another piece of paper. You do not draw on the tabs. Make the folds indicated on the diagram. Remember, a *mountain fold* is upward like a mountain 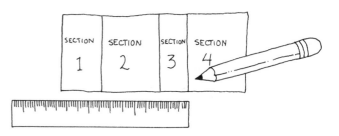. A *valley fold* is downward like a valley.

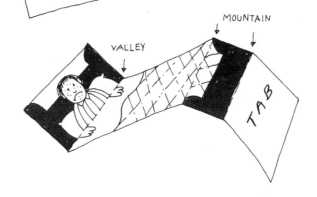

4 Apply glue on the front side of the tab. Fold the tab back and place it on the bottom section of your folded paper, with the edge of the tab on the fold line of the paper.

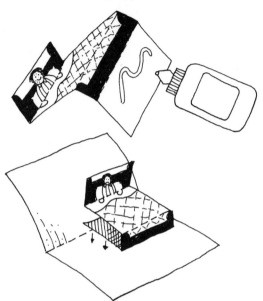

5 Apply glue behind the top section and close your card. Press down firmly. Wait for the glue to dry. Open the card carefully. The top section should now be glued in place. The figure or scene will collapse when the card is closed. It will pop open when the card is opened.

6 Decorate the front and inside of your card.

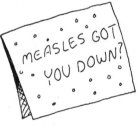

Other Ideas

You can make an animal or a figure pop out in the same way. Add a tab to the bottom of the figure. Fold the figure together with the tab into four sections. Glue it to your page.

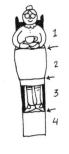

Make a Snake

1 Fold a heavy piece of paper, 21.5 cm x 14 cm (8½ in. x 5½ in.), in half. Put it aside. This will be your card.

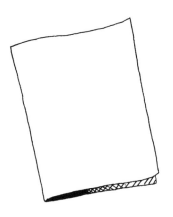

2 Take a heavy piece of paper, 10 cm x 10 cm (4 in. x 4 in.), and draw a spiral on it.

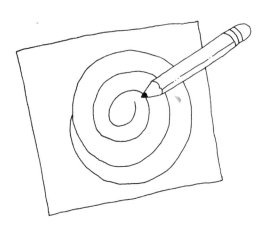

3 Turn the spiral into a snake, by adding eyes to the inside section. Colour your snake. You can add an interesting pattern to your colouring.

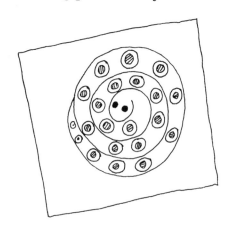

4 Cut out the spiral. Carefully decorate the back of the spiral.

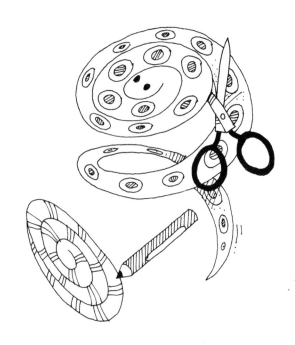

5 Apply glue behind the snake's head (centre of the spiral).

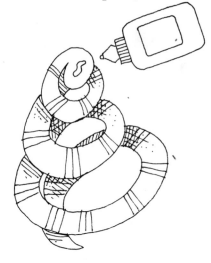

6 Place the whole snake in the middle of the left side of the folded page, glue side down. Allow the glue to dry.

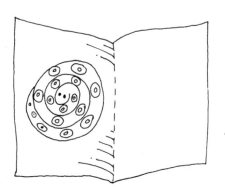

7 Apply a small amount of glue on the snake's tail (end of spiral). Close your card carefully and press it firmly. Allow the glue to dry. Open the card carefully. The tail should be glued in place.

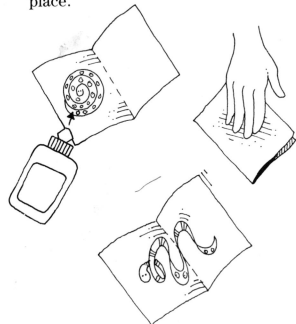

8 Add a tongue to your snake.

9 Decorate the front and inside of your card.

Cut-out Shapes

1 Fold a heavy piece of paper, 21.5 cm x 14 cm (8½ in. x 5½ in.), in half. Put it aside. This will be your card.

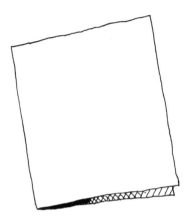

2 Cut a strip of paper, 21.5 cm x 7 cm (8½ in. x 2¾ in.). Fold it in half. Then accordion fold it. An *accordion fold* is an up-down-up fold or a down-up-down fold. Your strip should have three folds.

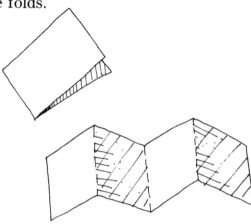

3 Close the strip and draw a figure on the top section. It can be a person, animal or object. Make sure that the hands or feet of your figure run off both sides of the section, so that your figures in each section will be connected.

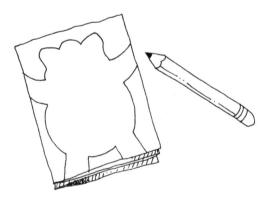

4 Cut and open the strip. The middle two figures should bend towards you. Colour the figures.

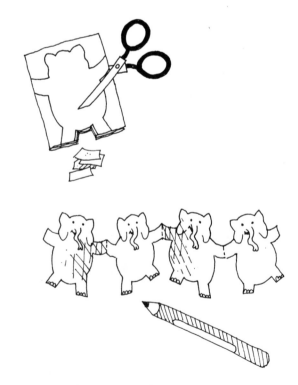

5 Fold the figures together again. Apply glue on the back of the far left figure and place it on the left side of your card, near the middle fold of your page. Press firmly and allow it to dry.

6 Apply glue on the back of the far right figure. Close your card and press firmly. The far right figure will now be glued to the right side of your card. Allow the glue to dry.

7 When you open your card, the middle two figures will be standing out.

8 Decorate the front and inside of your card.

Other Ideas

For an interesting Valentine card, make cut-out hearts and glue them inside a card. Make sure the sides of your hearts are connected.

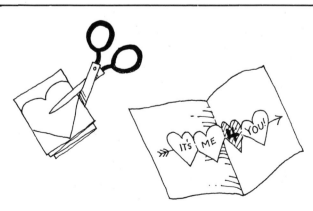

Make a Mountain or a Tent

1 Fold a heavy piece of paper, 21.5 cm x 14 cm (8½ in. x 5½ in.), in half. You will be making a mountain or tent with this paper.

2 Place the paper down, so that the fold is on your left. Mark a dot on the bottom edge of the page, 10 cm (4 in.) from the folded corner. Mark a dot on the folded edge, 10 cm (4 in.) up from the folded bottom corner. Using a ruler, draw a line between the dots.

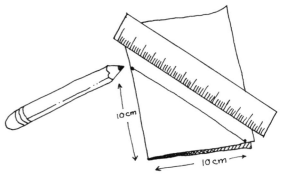

3 Cut along this line. Open the paper and you will have a triangle.

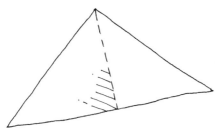

4 Place the triangle down so that the longest side is on the bottom. Fold the bottom edge up 1.2 cm (½ in.), so that your triangle looks like a hat.

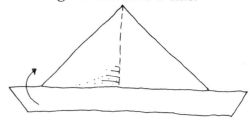

5 Fold the bottom edge down. Mark with a dot the spot where the fold lines meet. Starting at the dot, draw a little triangle at the bottom of your large triangle. Cut out the little triangle. You now have two tabs at the bottom of the mountain.

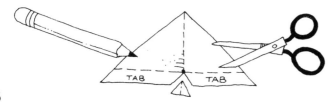

6 Fold a heavy piece of paper, 21.5 cm x 28 cm (8½ in. x 11 in.), in half. This will be the card base for your mountain or tent.

7 Place your card base so that the fold line is on the left. Take the top left corner and fold it over to make a large triangle. See the proportions on the diagram. Open your paper and you will see a large triangle.

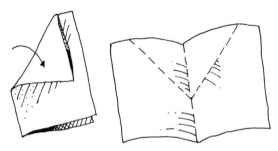

8 Now go back to your mountain paper. Fold the bottom tabs of your mountain in. Have the tabs meet in the centre (where you drew the dot) to form a mountain shape. Apply glue on the bottom of both tabs.

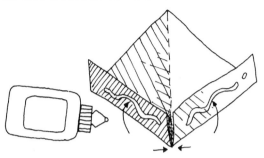

9 Fit the mountain shape into the large triangle on your card base. Glue the tabs of your mountain down along the triangle lines of your card base. The fold lines of the mountain should line up with the fold lines of the card base.

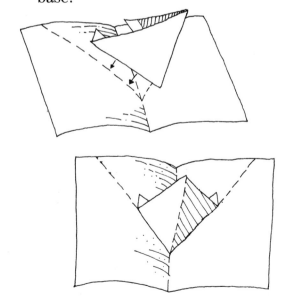

10 If you look at it one way, it looks like a mountain. Turn it around and it looks like a tent. Now decorate your mountain or tent. Add little figures if you wish. These scenes make good centrepieces for a table or a display.

Make a Trapeze

1 Fold a heavy piece of paper, 21.5 cm x 14 cm (8½ in. x 5½ in.), in half. Put it aside. This will be your card.

2 Cut two strips of heavy paper, each 12 cm x 7 cm (4¾ in. x 2¾ in.).

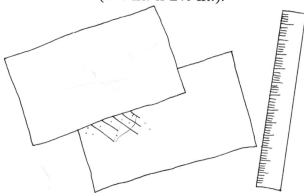

3 Fold both strips of paper in half lengthwise.

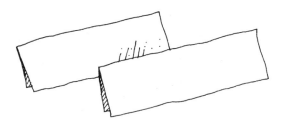

4 On the fold line of each strip, draw a line 4 cm (1½ in.) long. Open the paper and cut the line on both strips.

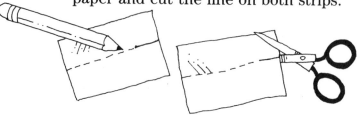

5 Refold one strip. Fold both sections back as far as you have cut. Turn the piece over and fold the other cut section back. If you turn your piece of paper around, you will have a T-shape.

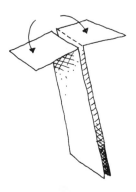

6 Apply glue in the middle of the long section of the T-shape and close the paper. Press firmly. Make another T-shape by repeating steps 5 and 6 with your second strip.

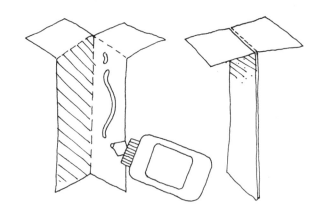

7 Open the folded heavy piece of paper you put aside. Place one T-shape near the bottom end of the paper, so that the centre of the T is lined up with the fold line of the paper. Place the other T-shape near the other end of the paper along the fold line. Glue both T-shapes to the paper.

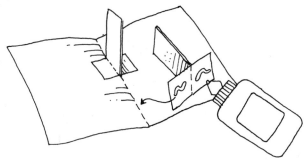

8 Now tape or glue the ends of a piece of string, a rubber band or a pipe-cleaner to the top of the T-shapes.

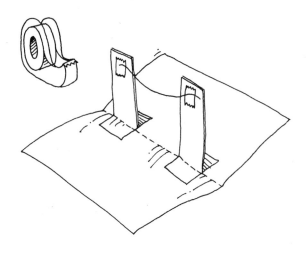

9 You can make a little man or woman swing on the string. Or you can make a little man or woman standing nearby, ready to jump.

Let's hang around together!

Sorry I couldn't make it.....

Other Ideas

You can make a person sitting on a swing. After you attach a pipe-cleaner or a long strip of paper to the tops of the T-shapes, add a swing and glue a little person to the swing.

I had a swinging time !!

Layered Bells or Angel's Dress

1 Fold a heavy piece of paper, 21.5 cm x 14 cm (8½ in. x 5½ in.), in half. Put it aside. This will be your card.

2 To make a bell pattern, take a piece of paper that is 10 cm x 14 cm (4 in. x 5½ in.). Fold it in half. Starting at the folded edge, draw half a bell. Cut out the shape and open it.

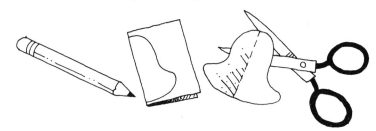

3 Take two pieces of paper, each 21.5 cm x 28 cm (8½ in. x 11 in.), each a different colour. Fold each paper in half. Then fold it in half again, so that your paper is divided into equal quarters. Lay your bell pattern on one folded paper and draw around it. Do the same with the other folded paper.

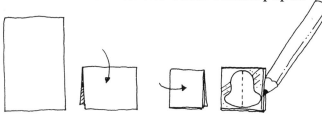

4 Cut the bell shape out of each folded paper. You should have eight bells altogether. Fold each bell shape in half.

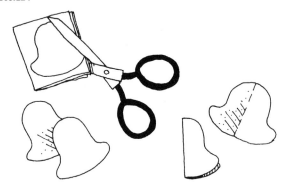

5 Open the bell shapes and put them in a pile, alternating their colours, for example: red, green, red, green and so on. Staple or sew the bell shapes along the fold line. If you staple the bells, make sure that the staples are directly on the fold line.

6 Apply glue on the bottom bell shape and place the pile of bell shapes in the middle of the heavy, folded piece of paper you have put aside. The fold lines should match. Allow the glue to dry.

7 Rip off 15 small pieces of cellophane tape. Now you are ready for your taping!

Here is the pattern for taping. Start with the left bell, Bell 1, which has been glued down to the card.

Tape: 1. Bell 1 and Bell 2 at bottom. For the first two bells, roll the tape so that it is sticky on both sides.
2. Bell 2 and Bell 3 in middle.
3. Bell 3 and Bell 4 at bottom.
4. Bell 4 and Bell 5 in middle.
5. Bell 5 and Bell 6 at bottom.
6. Bell 6 and Bell 7 in middle.
7. Bell 7 and Bell 8 at bottom. For the last bell, roll the tape so that it is sticky on both sides.

When you open the card, you should have a layered bell.

8 Decorate your card.

Other Ideas

Angel
You can use the bell shape as a dress for an angel. Draw an angel's head and wings.

Halloween Pumpkin
Instead of making a bell-shaped pattern, make a pumpkin-shaped pattern. Follow the instructions for the layered bell, using orange and yellow paper. When you are taping, you may want to use a lower piece of tape in the middle section.

Springs or Jacob's Ladder

1 Fold a heavy piece of paper, 21.5 cm x 14 cm (8½ in. x 5½ in.), in half. Put it aside. This will be your card.

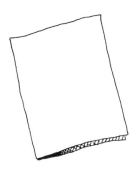

2 Draw, colour and cut out a little figure on a piece of paper, 5 cm x 5 cm (2 in. x 2 in.). It could be an animal or person. This will be your object. Put it aside.

3 Cut out two strips of paper, each 7 cm x 1 cm (2¾ in. x ¼ in.).

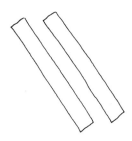

4 Apply glue at the end of one strip of paper. Lay the other strip at right angles to the first strip on the glued area. Allow the glue to dry.

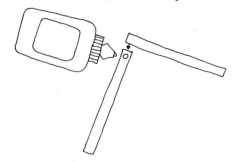

5 Bring the strip on the right side over to the left side and fold the edge. Bring the strip on the bottom up and over the glued area. Bring the strip on the left side over to the right side. Bring the strip on the top down to the bottom area. Continue overlapping the strips until all of the paper is folded.

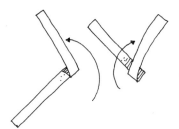 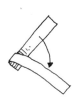 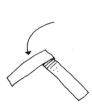

6 Apply glue under the top flap of paper and press the flap down. Cut off any extra paper.

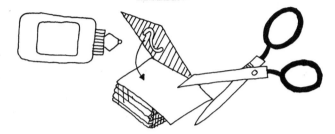

7 Pull the spring out slightly. Apply glue on one end of the spring and attach it to the back of the figure.

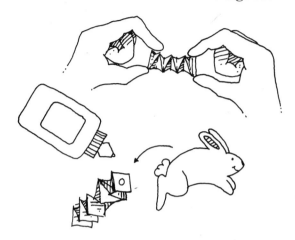

8 Apply glue on the other end of the spring and attach the figure with the spring to your card.

9 Decorate the rest of your card.

GUESS WHO'S BACK?

Other Ideas

If you make a large figure, you may want to make more than one spring to put under your figure.

HAPPY CHANUKAH!

More Springs

Man with a Concertina

1 Fold a heavy piece of paper, 21.5 cm x 14 cm (8½ in. x 5½ in.), in half. Put it aside. This will be your card.

2 Make a large spring using two strips of paper, each 2 cm x 28 cm (¾ in. x 11 in.).

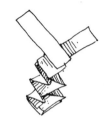

3 Glue one end of the spring .3 cm (⅛ in.) away from the middle fold line of your card.

4 Apply glue on the top part of the spring and close your card. Press the card firmly for about a minute.

5 Open the card and you will see a spring that is pulled open. This will be the concertina.

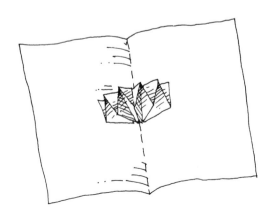

6 Draw a man around the concertina. Add some musical notes to the page. Open and close your card and the man will play his concertina.

Crown

1 Follow the instructions for the concertina. Instead of drawing a man, draw a face under the spring.

2 Decorate the crown by attaching stickers or sequins to the sides and top area of the spring.

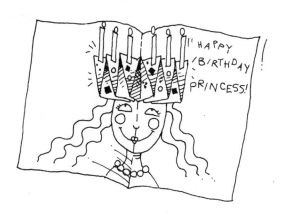

Holiday Decoration

1 Take two strips of paper, 54 cm x 4 cm (21¼ in. x 1½ in.), each a different colour. If necessary, you can glue strips of paper together to make the long strips. Make a spring with the strips.

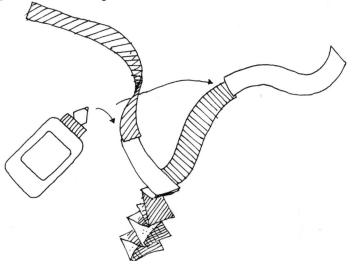

2 Apply glue on each end of the spring and attach both ends together. Add to your decoration with stickers and ribbons. Hang it on the wall, a Christmas tree or on a door.

Part Three **Push, Pull and Turn**

If you want to make a rocket slide upwards or a door fly open, you will enjoy Part Three. You will be making things move by pulling or pushing strips and by turning circles.

Part Three uses slots, sliding strips and circles to help make objects move by pulling, pushing and turning. You can make windows and doors that can be pushed and pulled open with your finger.

There are cards with slots, such as the "Go Fishing" card and the fire-breathing dragon. By pulling or pushing a strip of bristol board, you can make a rocket slide. You will enjoy the turning circle and the magic changing circle that changes one picture into another picture.

Tips

- Make cuts in the middle of a page with a cutting blade, such as an Olfa touch knife or an X-acto knife. Make sure an adult is around to supervise. If you don't have a cutting blade, you can use a pair of pointed scissors.
- Cut all lines as neatly as possible. If the cut line for the sliding strip has jagged edges, the sliding figure will catch on the paper.
- When you attach the outside card, make sure not to apply any glue on or near the sliding strip or turning circle. The sliding figure or circle will not move, if it is stuck to the outer card.
- Make sure that you create your circles away from the middle fold line of your page. Figures will not move or turn smoothly, if they are folded.

Window Cards

1 Take two pieces of paper, each 21.5 cm x 14 cm (8½ in. x 5½ in.). Put one paper aside.

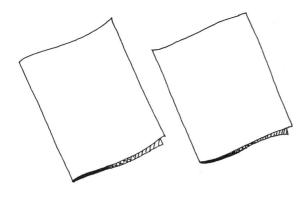

2 Draw a square that is 5 cm x 5 cm (2 in. x 2 in.) on the front of the other folded paper.

3 Cut three sides of the square with a cutting blade or a pair of pointed scissors, so that the window flaps open. It is easiest to make cuts in the middle of a page with a cutting blade. If you use scissors, puncture one of the corners of the square with the point of your scissors, and then start cutting very carefully. Fold the uncut side of the square towards the outside of the card.

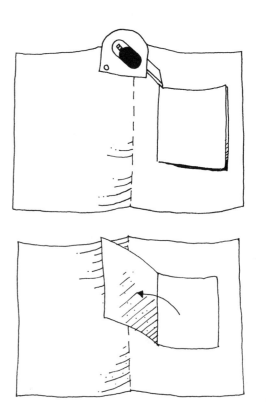

4 Apply glue to the inner side of your card. Place it over the paper you put aside, which now becomes the inside of your card. *Make sure you do not apply glue to the window area.*

5 Open your window and draw a little picture inside.

6 Decorate the rest of your card.

More Windows

Round Window

1 Draw a circle.

2 Cut the outline of the circle, except for a small section.

3 Fold the cut circle section back.

Heart Window

1 Draw a heart.

2 Cut the outline of the heart, except for one side.

3 Fold the cut heart section back.

Triangle Window

1 Draw a triangle.

2 Cut the outline of the triangle, except for one side.

3 Fold the cut section back.

Star Window

1 Draw a star.

2 Cut all of the star, except for one pointed end.

3 Fold the cut star section back.

Two-Door Window

1 Draw a rectangle with a line down the middle of the rectangle.

2 Cut all lines, except for both far sides of the rectangle.

3 Fold the cut sections back.

Go Fishing!

1 Take a piece of paper, 8 cm x 5 cm (3⅛ in. x 2 in.). On the paper, draw a fish with a tab under the tail. The top and bottom of the fish should not reach the edges of the paper.

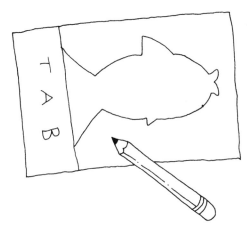

2 Cut out your fish and write a message on it. Colour the rest of the fish. Glue, tape or tie a short piece of string to the mouth of your fish.

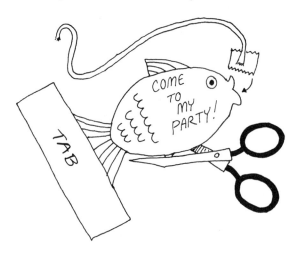

3 Fold two pieces of paper, each 21.5 cm x 14 cm (8½ in. x 5½ in.), in half. Put one aside.

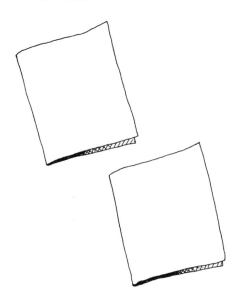

4 Take the other paper and open it up. On the right side of the paper, draw a horizontal line, 4 cm (1½ in.), near the top of the page. The line should be larger than the fish, but smaller than the tab. Cut the line with a cutting blade or a pair of pointed scissors to make the slot. A *slot* is an opening that is like a pocket.

5 Put the fish behind the slot and pull the string through the slot. Take a strip of heavy paper, 5 cm x 1 cm (2 in. x ¼ in.), and make a little fishing pole. Write on it: "Go fishing!" Glue, tape or tie the string to the fishing pole.

6 Apply glue to the back of the inside card. Make sure you apply glue around the edges and around the fold of the inside card. *Do not apply glue near the slot or the fish.*

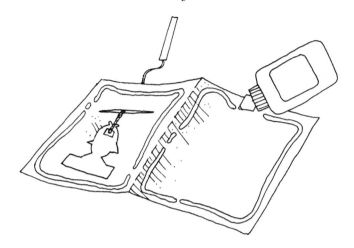

7 Place the card inside the paper you put aside, which now becomes the outside of your card.

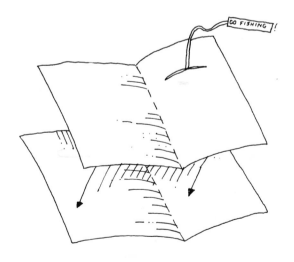

8 Decorate the front and inside of your card. When you open the card and pull on the fishing line, you will pull out your message.

Make a Rocket

1 Take two pieces of paper, each 21.5 cm x 28 cm (8½ in. x 11 in.). Fold each paper in half. Put one aside.

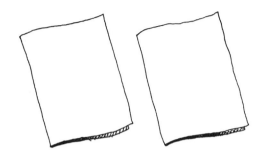

2 Open your other piece of paper. Draw a long line, about 10 cm (4 in.), diagonally across the right side. Cut this line with a cutting blade or with a pointed pair of scissors. This is your large slot. Cut a small vertical slot, 3 cm (1⅛ in.) long, near the end of the large slot.

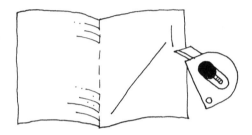

3 Draw a rocket or a space shuttle on a heavy piece of paper, 5 cm x 5 cm (2 in. x 2 in.). The rocket or space shuttle should be about 4 cm (1½ in.) long. Colour it and cut it out.

4 Now make a sliding strip that will help your rocket move across the page. To make the strip, cut a piece of bristol board or cardboard, 14 cm x 2 cm (5½ in. x ¾ in.).

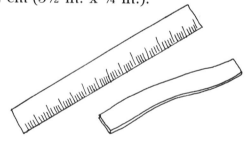

5 On a small piece of heavy paper, cut a tab, 4 cm x 1 cm (1½ in. x ¼ in.). Glue the bottom half of the tab to the left side of your strip. Fold the rest of the tab down on itself.

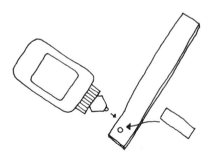

6 Slip the strip through the small slot. Pull the loose part of the tab through the large slot. Fold the end of the tab upward on the tab's fold line. Make sure the fold line of your tab is on the large slot.

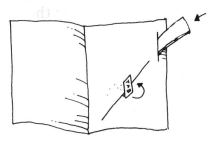

7 Apply glue to the top of your folded tab. Place your rocket on the folded tab. *Make sure you do not glue your rocket to the card.* Allow the glue to dry before you pull the strip.

8 Cut the end of the strip to make it shorter if necessary. Your rocket should now move easily up and down the large slot of your card.

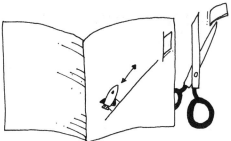

9 Carefully apply glue around the edges of the back of your card away from the slots. *Make sure you do not apply glue near the slots, the strip or the rocket.* Place your card on top of the paper you put aside. Press firmly.

10 Decorate the front and inside of your card.

CONGRATULATIONS ☆ ON YOUR GRADUATION ☾ ⊕ ☉ ∘ ☆

MAY YOU CONTINUE TO REACH NEW HEIGHTS! ☾

Fire-breathing Dragon

1 Take two pieces of paper, each 21.5 cm x 28 cm (8½ in. x 11 in.). Fold each paper in half. Put one aside.

2 Draw a ferocious dragon on the right side of your other paper. Its mouth should be wide open.

3 Cut a sliding strip of bristol board, 11 cm x 2 cm (4¼ in. x ¾ in.). Draw and cut the end of the strip so that it looks like shooting flames. The flames should be about 5 cm (2 in.) long. Colour the flames red and orange. If you wish, you can write a message on the end of the strip and colour around the message.

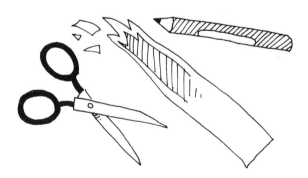

4 Cut a small slot, 1 cm (⅜ in.) long, at the dragon's mouth to fit the flame end of the strip. Measure 5 cm (2 in.) from the small slot towards the right side of the page. Draw and cut a larger slot, 2.5 cm (1 in.). The two slots should be parallel to each other.

5 Turn the card over. Fit the large end of the fire-strip through the large slot. Fit the flame end of the strip through the smaller slot.

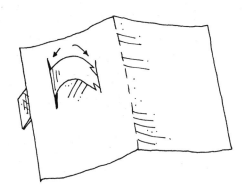

6 Turn to the front of the card. If you push the strip forwards, the flame will shoot out of the dragon's mouth. Do not pull the strip too far or the strip will come out of the small slot.

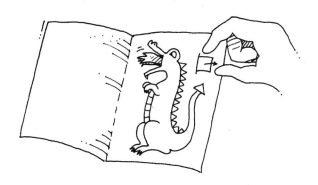

7 Now, carefully apply glue around the edges of the back of the card away from the slots. Place your card on top of the paper you put aside. Press firmly.

8 Decorate the front and inside of your card.

More Sliding Strips

Talking Mouth with a Sliding Tongue

1 Make a card with a talking mouth. (See pages 22 and 23, steps 1 to 9.) *Do not glue the front of the card to your talking mouth yet.*

2 To make the sliding strip, cut a strip of bristol board, 15 cm x 1 cm (6 in. x ¼ in.). Cut a piece of red construction paper that is shaped like a tongue. The tongue should be about 5 cm (2 in.) long and 1 cm (⅜ in.) wide. Fold the tongue in half and glue the bottom half to one end of your strip.

3 On the right side of the fold line, 5 cm (2 in.) below the bottom of the mouth, cut a slot that is 2 cm (¾ in.). The slot should be 1.2 cm (½ in.) from the fold line.

4 Insert the bottom of the strip through the slot at the back of your card. Push the tongue through the back of the open mouth.

5 Apply glue around the edge of the back of your card. *Make sure that you do not apply glue near the slot.* Now glue your card to the paper that you put aside, which now becomes the outside of your card. When you pull the strip up and down, the tongue will move in the mouth.

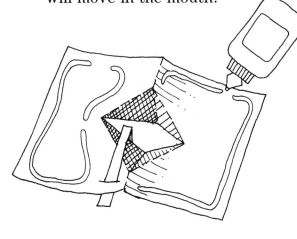

6 Decorate the front of your card.

Make a Door That Flaps Open

1 Take two pieces of heavy paper, each 21.5 cm x 28 cm (8½ in. x 11 in.). Fold each paper in half. Put one aside.

2 On the right side of the card, draw two vertical lines, each 2 cm (¾ in.) long. The two lines should be 10 cm (4 in.) apart. Label the left slot "A" and the right slot "B". Cut them with a cutting blade or a pointed pair of scissors.

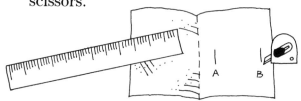

3 Cut a strip of bristol board, 18 cm x 2 cm (7 in. x ¾ in.).

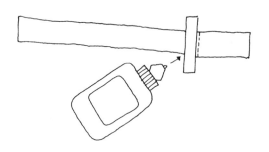

4 Starting at the right side of this strip, measure 4 cm (1½ in.). Fold at this line.

5 Cut out a thin rectangle of bristol board, 4 cm x .5 cm (1½ in. x ¼ in.). Glue the strip against the left side of the fold line. Press firmly and allow the glue to dry.

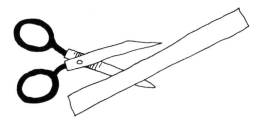

6 Insert the short end of the strip into slot A, so that the thin rectangle is facing out.

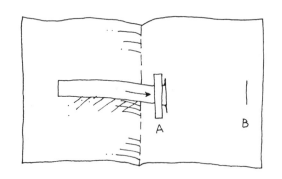

7 Hold the thin rectangle down. Fold the long end of the strip over the thin rectangle and insert the end of it into slot B.

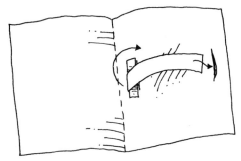

8 Apply glue around the edges of the card away from the strip. *Be careful not to apply any glue near the strip.* Place the card on the paper you put aside. Press firmly.

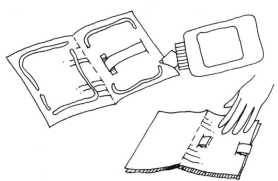

9 Turn the card over. Mark the left end of the strip flap "C" and the right end of the strip "PULL".

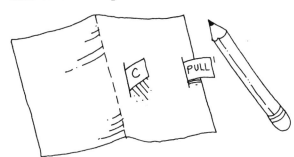

10 To make the door, cut a piece of paper, 7.6 cm x 5 cm (3 in. x 2 in.). Fold it in half. Cover the inside with glue on both sides.

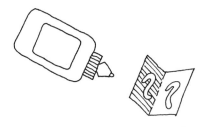

11 Fold the paper over flap C to form a door. Press the edges of the door firmly. Push and pull the strip to make the door open and close.

12 Now make a drawing under the flapping door and on the rest of the page.

Turning Circle

1 Take two pieces of paper, each 21.5 cm x 14 cm (8½ in. x 5½ in.). Fold each paper in half. Put one aside.

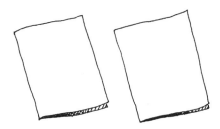

2 Take another piece of paper, 10 cm x 10 cm (4 in. x 4 in.). On this paper, trace something that is round, such as a glass, cup or the lid of a can. The diameter of the circle should be about 6 to 8 cm (2¼ to 3⅛ in.). Cut out the circle. Mark the middle of the circle with a dark dot.

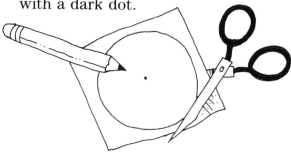

3 Place the circle under the right side of your card. The edge of the circle should be just outside the edge of your page.

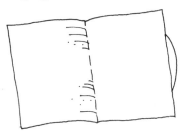

4 Hold the paper, with the circle behind it, up to a light or against a window. You should see the dot from the middle of the circle. Mark it with a dot on your paper.

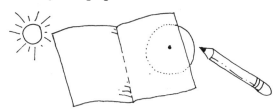

5 Draw a small window, 1.6 cm x 1.6 cm (⅝ in. x ⅝ in.), on the paper. Draw the window 1 cm (¼ in.) above the dot. Cut out the window using either a cutting blade or pointed scissors.

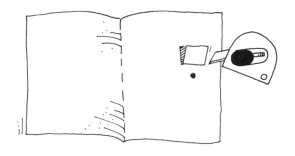

6 Make a small hole in the middle of the circle. Make another small hole on the dot below the window of your page. Take a small brass paper fastener and put it through first the hole in the paper, then the hole in the circle. Close the fastener.

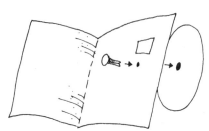

7 Draw a picture on the part of the circle that shows through the window. Turn the circle and draw another picture. Continue doing this until your turning circle has 4 or 5 pictures.

8 Turn the card over. Apply glue around the edge of the paper, away from the circle area. Carefully put the paper you have put aside on top of the glued card. Press firmly. When you turn the circle, you will see a changing picture inside your window. This changing scene can be used as either the outside or the inside of your card.

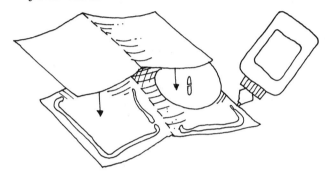

9 Decorate the front and inside of your card.

Changing Circle

1 Take a heavy piece of paper, 21.5 cm x 28 cm (8½ in. x 11 in.), and fold it in half. Put it aside.

2 Trace and cut out the pattern pieces on page 77 for the changing circle. Trace patterns A and B on one colour of heavy paper. Trace patterns C and D and the Stop pattern on another colour of heavy paper. Don't forget to mark tabs and flaps "A", "B", "C", "D" and "STOP" on your pieces in erasable pencil.

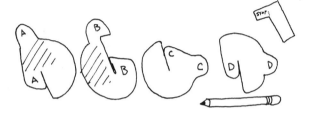

3 Take pieces A and B. Interlock them by putting flap B into flap A.

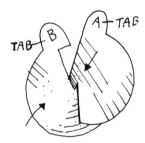

4 Take pieces C and D. Interlock them by putting flap D into flap C.

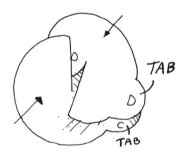

5 Turn circle AB, so that the round tab B is pointing upwards. Draw a picture on the interlocking circle. If you are making a sad face changing to a happy face, draw a happy face on this circle. This circle will be your bottom circle.

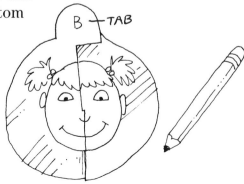

6 Lay circle CD down, so that the tab D is on your right. Draw a picture on the interlocking circle. If you are making a sad face changing to a happy face, draw a sad face on this circle. This circle will be your top circle.

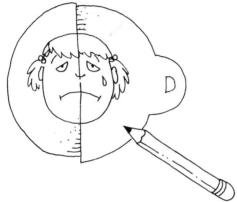

7 To put together the changing circle, first take apart circle CD. Then hold circle AB, so that the tab B is at the bottom. Holding tab B with your left hand, take piece D with your right hand and slide flap D into the top of circle AB. Piece D should now cover piece B.

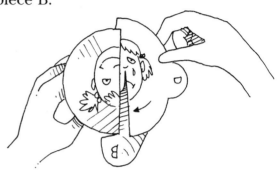

8 Hold the circle with your right hand. With your left hand, slide flap C up and under tab B. Piece C should now cover piece A. Tabs C and D should overlap. Tabs A and B should overlap.

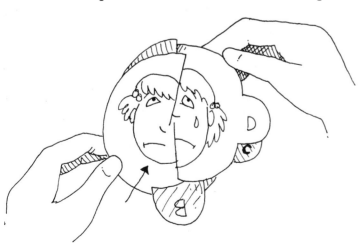

9 Glue tabs A and B together. Glue tabs C and D together. *Be careful not to apply any glue in the circle area.*

10 Open the paper that you have put aside. Tape tab D to the right side of your paper.

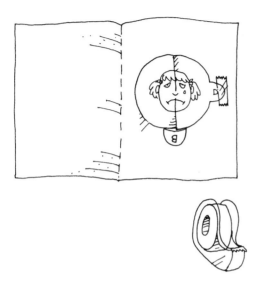

11 Take the Stop piece and fold the Stop tab against the rest of the strip. Apply glue under the lined strip but *not* under the Stop tab.

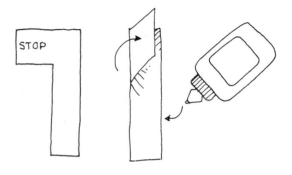

12 Put the glued strip over tab D. Lift up the Stop flap and fold over the circle. Make sure that your circle turns freely.

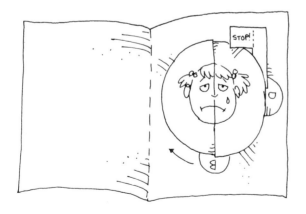

13 Now turn tab B up and around to the Stop flap. *Do not go beyond the Stop flap or your circle will fall apart.* Your sad face will change to a happy face.

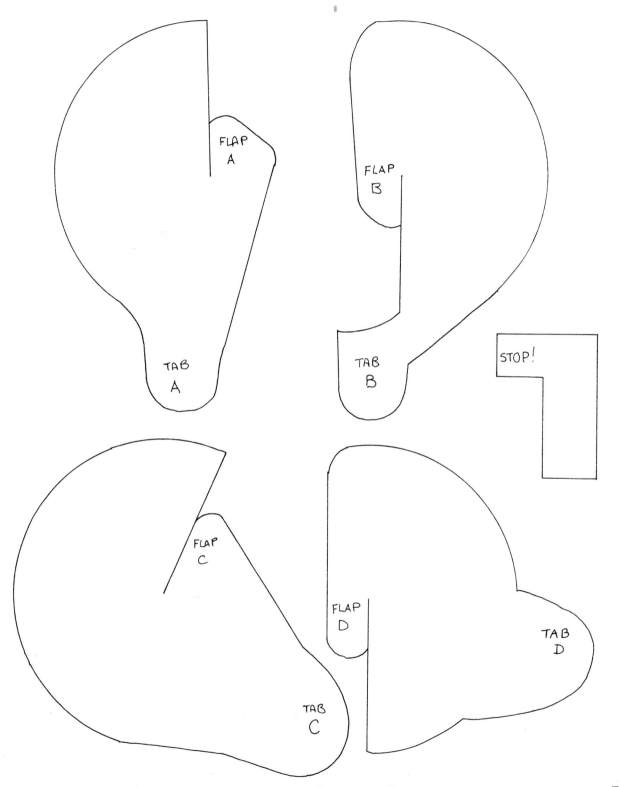

FLAP
A

FLAP
B

STOP!

TAB
A

TAB
B

FLAP
C

FLAP
D

TAB
D

TAB
C

Part Four **Combining Ideas**

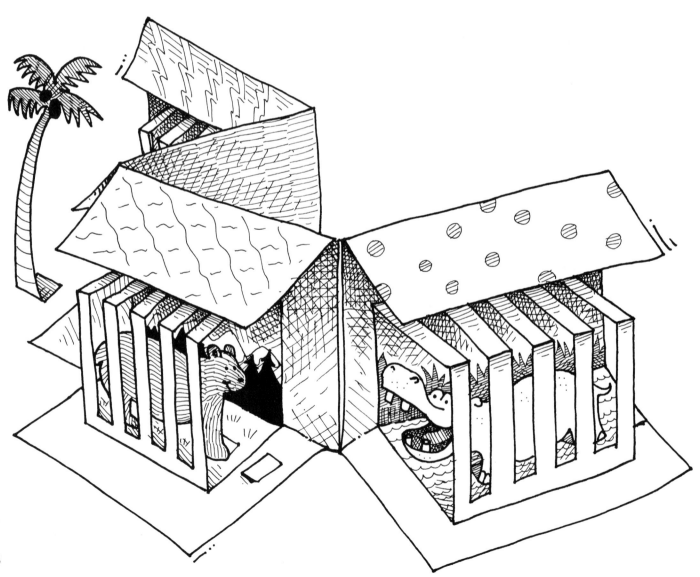

The activities in Part Four will give you hours of challenge and fun. You will enjoy combining the many pop-up ideas that you have learned in this book.

The old-fashioned zoo is a great project to make with a friend. Together or on your own, you can cut out cages, find pictures of animals and decorate your zoo. The pop-up zoo makes a wonderful gift or centrepiece.

Creating a pop-up book is exciting, because you can combine your favourite pop-up ideas in one book. With this project, you will be writing a story, making pop-up pages and making a hard cover for your book.

Tips

- The two projects in Part Four take more time to make than the activities in the first three sections. Plan on working for two or three sessions before finishing your zoo or book.
- Make sure that you use a heavy paper for making your zoo. One type of paper that is excellent is called Mayfair Coverstock. It is available at many art supply stores.
- Use a glue stick for gluing your pop-up book together.
- Be patient! Although these projects require more time, you will cherish the results for many years.

Make an Old-fashioned Zoo or Pet Shop

1 Take eight pieces of heavy paper, each 21.5 cm x 28 cm (8½ in. x 11 in.). Make the front sections of four cages, following the instructions on page 34. Put the other four pieces of paper aside. They will be the back cards for your cages.

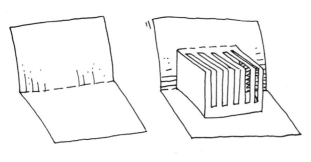

2 On the bottom right side of each cage, cut a slot, 2 cm (¾ in.) long, near the edge of the cage. This slot will be for your sliding strip.

3 Now glue on the back cards for each cage. *Do not apply glue in the area of the cage slots.* Put your four cages aside.

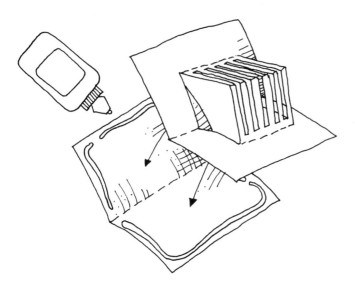

4 To make the animals for your cages, find pictures in old magazines or draw them yourself on heavy paper. Make sure your animals are not taller than 5 cm (2 in.). If you are using magazines, glue the magazine pictures to heavy paper and cut them out.

5 To make the *sliding strips* for your figures, cut out four strips of bristol board, each 15 cm x 1.5 cm (6 in. x ½ in.).

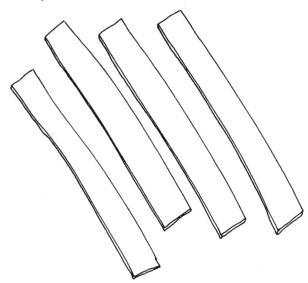

6 Make four *tabs* for the sliding strips by cutting four pieces of heavy paper, 2½ cm x 1 cm (1 in. x ⅜ in.). Fold the tabs in half. Glue one tab onto the bottom left corner of each of the strips. Put the sliding strips with tabs aside.

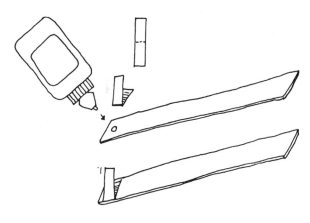

7 To make four hinges that hold the cages together, take eight pieces of heavy paper, each 21.5 cm x 14 cm (8½ in. x 5½ in.). From the top left corner of one piece of paper, measure 7.6 cm (3 in.) to the right, and mark it with a dot. From the bottom left corner, measure 7.6 cm (3 in.) to the right, and mark it with a dot. With a ruler, draw a line from one dot to the other dot. Repeat these measurements with three other pieces of paper. You will now have four papers with lines and four blank papers.

8 On one paper with a line, apply glue to the larger area to the right of the line. Place another piece of paper without a line on the glued area of the first paper. Take the top left flap of paper that is not glued and fold it back in a *valley fold* over the glued area. Turn the paper over and fold the other flap back the same distance in a *valley fold*. Now you have a hinge. Repeat this with the other papers, until you have four hinges.

9 Now attach the hinges. Take two cages and place them side by side. Take one hinge and put it down to look like a T. Apply glue on the two inside flaps of your hinge. Put the hinge between the two cages. Press the glued flap on the left to the back of the cage on the left. Press the glued flap on the right to the back of the cage on the right. The hinge will now hold the two cages together.

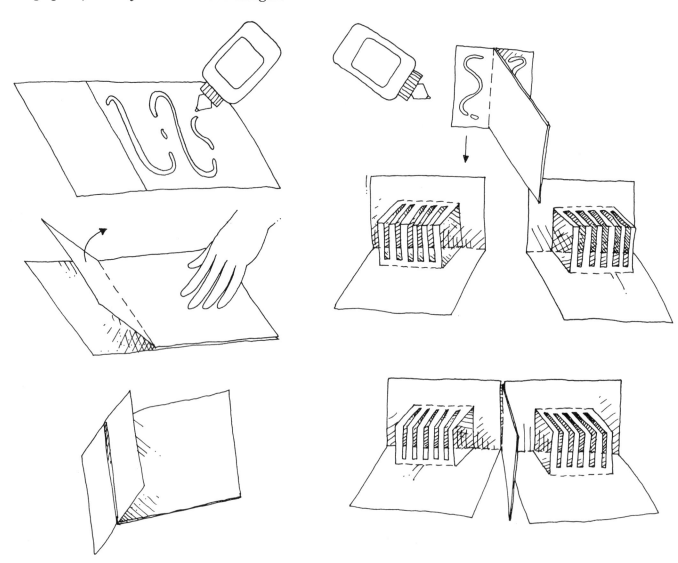

10 Working towards the right, attach two more hinges in the same way to the cages, so that all four cages are joined together.

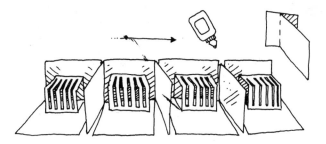

11 Take the fourth hinge and glue the left flap to the back of the fourth cage. The right flap of the hinge remains without glue. Cut sections from the top and bottom of the right flap, 4 cm (1½ in.) long and 7.6 cm (3 in.) wide to make a tab.

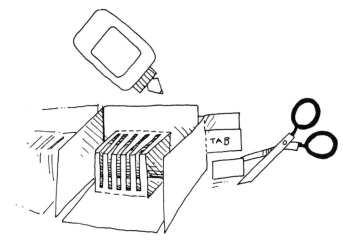

12 To make awnings for your cages, take four pieces of paper, 21.5 cm x 28 cm (8½ in. x 11 in.). Fold them in half. Take one and place it down so that the folded edge is at the top. Starting at the top left folded corner, measure down the edge 7 cm (2¾ in.) and mark a dot. Do the same for the top right corner. Draw a line from one dot to the other dot and cut the paper along this line. Repeat these instructions with the other three pieces of paper until you have four awnings.

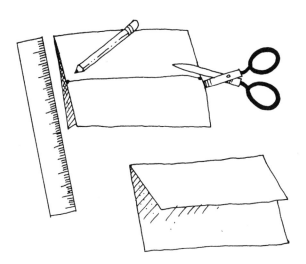

13 Now attach the awnings. Apply glue on the larger area of the awning facing you. Attach the awning to the back of the first cage. It should cover the hinges and the back of the cage exactly. The front flap of the awning will be hanging over the cage. Attach the other three awnings to the other three cages in the same way.

14 Now put your animals in their cages. Slide the end of one strip with the tab through the slot and into the cage. Carefully apply glue on the front of the tab and attach an animal. Insert the other sliding strips in the same way, until all of the animals are in their cages. When you pull the strips, they will move.

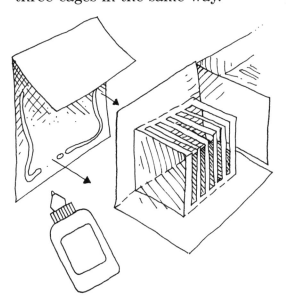

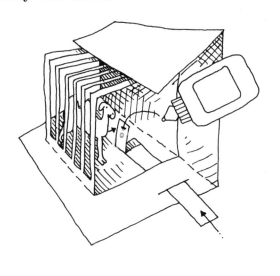

15 Decorate your cages and hinges by adding drawings, paintings or other materials.

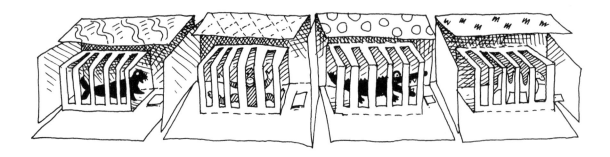

16 To set up the cages as a centrepiece for your table, fold the hinges, so that the cages are in a square facing outwards. Take your scissors and gently insert the ends of the scissors between the awning and the cage on the left side of the first cage. This will create an opening for the tab that is on the last cage. When the tab is slipped into the opening, the square of cages will be complete!

17 To fold up the cages, lay the cages so that they are on their backs. Fold up the bottoms and then fold down the awnings. Starting on the left side, fold the cages towards the right. Fold the hinges towards the right as well. Fold the last hinge towards the left before folding up the last cage. Only your tab will now be sticking out. Take a piece of tape and roll it so that it is sticky on both sides. Put it under the tab and it will hold your zoo cages in place. You will now have a nice self-contained wallet which holds your zoo. Remember to remove the tape when setting up your cages again.

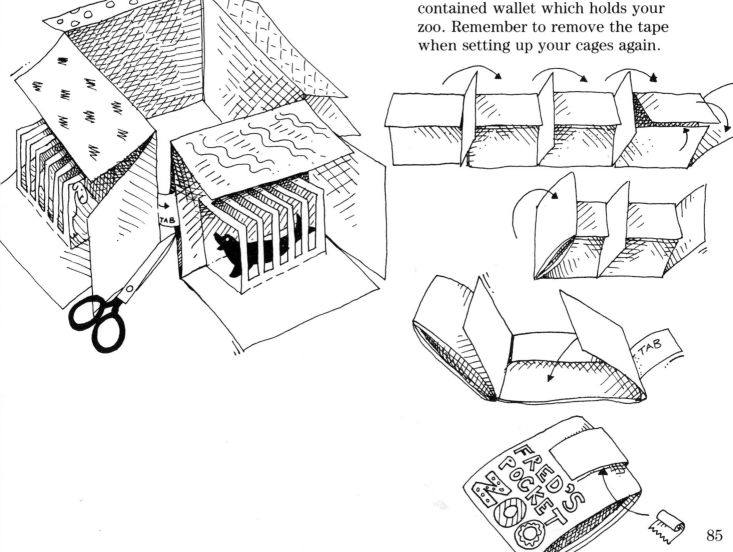

Make Your Own Pop-up Book

Making a pop-up book is fun, because you have to use pop-up ideas that suit the scenes in your story. For instance, if you think about the story Little Red Riding Hood, you could have the following pop-up scenes in your book:

Little Red Riding Hood leaving her house.

Use a sliding strip (page 68).

Little Red Riding Hood going into her grandmother's cottage.

Use a flapping door (page 70).

The wolf thinking to himself that he will follow her.

Use a turning circle (page 72).

The wolf dressed up as the grandmother in bed.

Use a talking mouth (page 22).

Make the inside of your book.

1 Write a rough draft of your story:
- Keep your story short and simple.
- Divide your story into four or five sections of text, each with no more than three or four sentences.
- Choose one pop-up idea for each section of your story.

2 Rewrite or type each section of your story on separate strips of paper, each 21.5 cm x 7 cm (8½ in. x 2¾ in.). In pencil, number them in sequence. Each strip will be the text for one double-page spread in your final book.

3 Put aside twice as many sheets of paper, each 21.5 cm x 28 cm (8½ in. x 11 in.), as you have strips. To start your first pop-up page, fold two papers in half. Put one aside.

4 Decide whether you want your book to open at the side or at the bottom. If you are making a talking mouth in your book, it should open at the *side*. If you are making a fold-and-fit-in bed or a person giving a hug, you should have your book opening at the *bottom*.

A book opening at the bottom:
Place your paper down so that the sides that are 21.5 cm (8½ in.) long are at the top and bottom. Glue your first text strip along the bottom or top of your page.

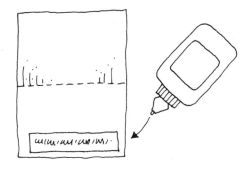

A book opening at the side:
Place your paper down so that the sides that are 28 cm (11 in.) long are at the top and bottom. Glue your first text strip along the bottom or top of your page.

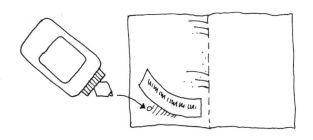

5 On your double-spread page, make a pop-up to go with the first section of your story. Each page in your book will be like one pop-up card.

6 Complete the page by doing drawings or painting around the pop-up and the text. You have finished the first double-spread page of your book!

7 Take the folded paper that you have set aside. Glue it to your pop-up page, pressing firmly.

8 Make the rest of your pages in the same way. Fold each page in half and stack them in order, so that the first page is at the top of the stack, and so on.

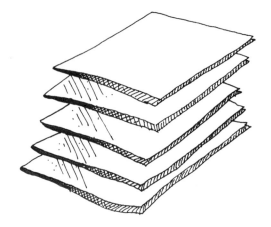

9 Glue your pages together. Apply glue (preferably with a glue stick) between the first folded page and the second folded page, making sure that they are glued as evenly as possible. Continue gluing the rest of the folded pages together in the same way.

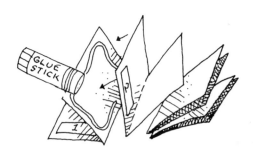

10 Now make your title page and end page. Take two more pieces of paper, 21.5 cm x 28 cm (8½ in. x 11 in.). Fold each paper in half. Take one folded paper and glue it on the top of your stack of pages. Take the other folded paper and glue it to the bottom of your stack of pages.

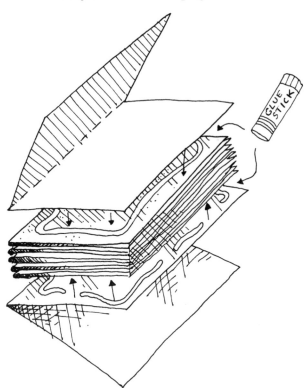

11 Open your book. The left page should be blank. The right side is your *title page*. Write the title of your story, your name and the year. Give yourself a publishing name. Decorate the page. Write a dedication on the left page, if you wish.

12 Open to the back of your book. On the left page, write about yourself under the heading, "About the Author." Add a photograph of yourself. On the right page, you can make a library card or a page for "Comments" from your friends. *Remember not to decorate the top or bottom pages of your stack, since they will be glued to the hard cover.*

Make a hard cover for your book.

1 Take a piece of heavy paper, 36 cm x 28 cm (14 in. x 11 in.). From each corner of your paper, measure 2.5 cm (1 in.) and mark the measurements with dots. Join all the dots that are across the page from each other. You will now have four lines around the inside edges of your page.

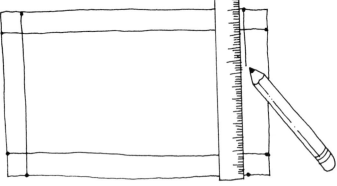

2 Take two pieces of bristol board, 23 cm x 4.6 cm (9 in. x 5¾ in.). Put one aside. Apply glue to one side of the other board, preferably with a glue stick. Place the glued side of the bristol board down within the lines on the left side of your paper. *Make sure that the top left corner of the bristol board lines up perfectly with the top left corner of the drawn lines on the paper.* Press firmly.

3 Glue the other bristol board to the right side of your paper. *Make sure that the top right corner of the bristol board lines up perfectly with the top right corner of the drawn lines.* Press firmly.

4 Apply glue to the back of a strip of bristol board, 23 cm x .6 cm (9 in. x ¼ in.). Place it exactly between the two pieces of bristol board, so that there is a slight space on either side of the strip.

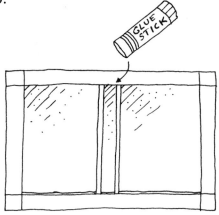

5 With a ruler and pencil, draw lines diagonally across the corners. The lines should come within .6 cm (¼ in.) of the corners of the bristol board. Cut along these lines until all of the corners are removed from the page.

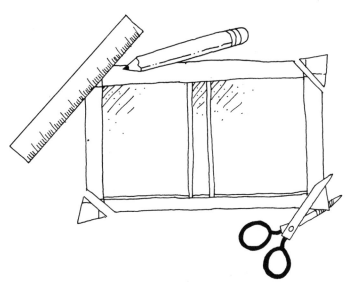

6 Draw a W-shape on the paper above the top end of the bristol board strip. The two bottom points of the W-shape should point to each corner of the strip. Cut out the two outside triangles of the W-shape. Do the same at the bottom end of the strip with an M-shape. There should now be a paper triangle at each end of the bristol board strip.

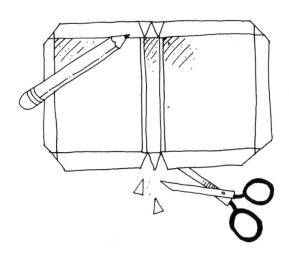

7 Carefully score the paper along the edges of the bristol board and fold the paper along the score lines. Apply glue under the top flaps and the top triangle. Firmly press the flaps and the triangle against the bristol board. Do the same with the bottom flaps and the bottom triangle. Finally, put glue under the side flaps and press them down firmly.

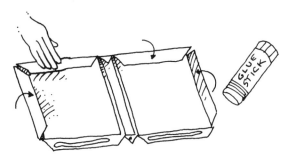

8 Fold the book through the middle, to make the *spine* of your book. Carefully place a piece of cloth or plastic tape, 28 cm (11 in.) long, evenly along the spine of your book. Fold the remaining ends of the tape over the inside of the cover.

9 Now lay the stack of glued pages on the inside of the cover, so that the folded edges of the stack fit into the middle of the bristol board strip. Apply glue to the top page of the stack, preferably with a glue stick. Holding the stack firmly with one hand, so that the folded edges of paper are lined up with the spine, tilt the right side of the book towards the left. Press the glued page to the left area of the inside cover. Smooth the page with your hand. Allow the glue to dry.

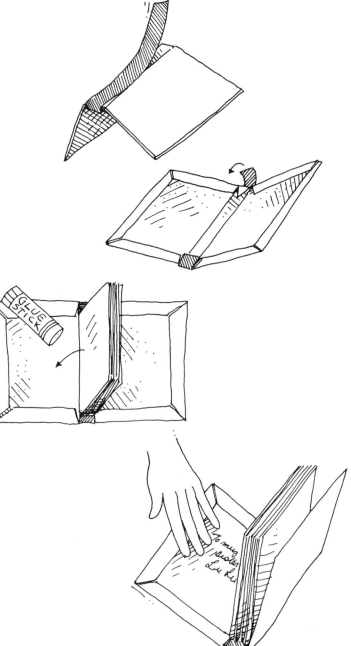

10 Apply glue to the back page. Tilt the left side of the book towards the right. Press the glued page to the right area of the inside cover. Now your book is glued together.

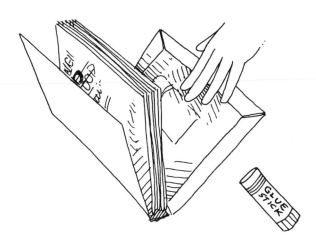

11 Decorate the front and back covers of your book.

About the Author

Joan Irvine, known to hundreds of Canadian children as "The Pop-Up Lady," was born in Wiarton, Ontario, Canada. She has worked as a Montessori teacher and has published several natural activity books in Canada. She spends her time giving pop-up workshops in schools and libraries and editing *Buzz*, a children's magazine. Joan Irvine lives in Wiarton, Ontario.

J   Irvine, Joan
745.54   How to make pop-ups
Irv